D1299325

WITHDRAWN

Markham Public Libraries
Unionville Library
FEB   2007   15 Library Lane
Unionville, ON L3R 5C4

CANADIAN FUR TRADE

FORTS and TRADING POSTS

Bev Cline

Weigl

CALGARY

www.weigl.com

Published by Weigl Educational Publishers Limited
6325 – 10 Street SE
Calgary, Alberta, Canada
T2H 2Z9

Website: www.weigl.com

Copyright ©2007 WEIGL EDUCATIONAL PUBLISHERS LIMITED
All rights reserved. No part of this publication may be reproduced,
stored in a retrieval system, or transmitted in any form or by any
means, electronic, mechanical, photocopying, recording, or otherwise,
without the prior written permission of the publisher.

Library and Archives Canada Cataloguing in Publication

Cline, Beverly Fink, 1951-
Forts and trading posts / Bev Cline.
(Canadian fur trade)
Includes index.
ISBN 1-55388-214-8 (bound).—ISBN 1-55388-215-6 (pbk.)

1. Trading posts—Canada—History—Juvenile literature.
2. Fortification—Canada—History—Juvenile literature. 3. Fur
trade—Canada—History--Juvenile literature. I. Title. II. Series.
FC3206.C44 2006   j971   C2006-902477-4

Printed in the United States of America
1 2 3 4 5 6 7 8 9 0 10 09 08 07 06

We acknowledge the financial support of the Government of Canada
through the Book Publishing Industry Development Program (BPIDP)
for our publishing activities.

Photograph and Text Credits
Library and Archives Canada: page 28 (C-001918); **Mary Evans
Picture Library:** pages 17, 25; **Northwind Picture Archives:**
page 19.

Every reasonable effort has been made to trace ownership and to
obtain permission to reprint copyright material. The publishers would
be pleased to have any errors or omissions brought to their attention
so that they may be corrected in subsequent printings.

Project Coordinator
Heather C. Hudak

Designer
Terry Paulhus

All of the Internet URLs given
in the book were valid at the
time of publication. However,
due to the dynamic nature of
the Internet, some addresses
may have changed, or sites
may have ceased to exist
since publication. While the
author and publisher regret
any inconvenience this
may cause readers, no
responsibility for
any such changes can be
accepted by either the
author or the publisher.

CONTENTS

Introduction 5

Building a Network 7

Inside the Trading Post 8

Life at the Trading Post 10

Defending the Posts 12

The North West Company 14

Important Forts 16

Aboriginal Peoples and the Trading Posts 18

How Women Contributed 20

Fur Trade Personalities 22

The Rise and Fall of the Beaver 24

The Fur Trade Today 26

Timeline 28

Test Your Knowledge 30

More Information 31

Words to Know/Index 32

Throughout the 1700s, the French and British battled for control of Louisbourg, which was a major trading post in Nova Scotia.

Introduction

In the 1600s, the wide-brimmed felt hat made from beaver fur became a status symbol in Europe. Everyone who could afford one wanted such a hat. Beavers were plentiful in Canada. Several countries raced to supply the growing European market for furs. Although beaver fur was the most popular, there also was demand for fox and marten fur.

During the fur trade, Aboriginal Peoples traded furs for European goods. At first, fur traders traded along the St. Lawrence River and on the Grand Banks of what is now Newfoundland and Labrador. As Europeans demanded more fur, the traders journeyed farther and farther into the interior of Canada. They explored mountains, rivers, and bays. As they canoed and **portaged** farther west and north, they established strong trade relations with the Aboriginal Peoples. To support this trade, the fur traders built a network of trading posts along the country's rivers.

Many of these trading posts were the beginnings of towns and cities familiar to us today, including Edmonton, Victoria, and Winnipeg.

Hudson's Bay Price List

During the fur trade, beaver pelts were the main currency. Aboriginal traders would "buy" European goods using beaver pelts.

Trade Goods	Cost
1 gun	14 beaver pelts
5 pounds (2.2 kg) gunpowder	1 beaver pelt
1 hatchet	1 beaver pelt
1 yard (1m) cloth	3 beaver pelts
1 pound (0.5 kg) tobacco	2 beaver pelts
4 knives	1 beaver pelt
1 kettle	1 1/2 beaver pelts
1 large roll of string	1 1/4 beaver pelts

Explorers and fur traders could only navigate Hudson Bay during the summer months, before the water froze.

Building a Network

In the early part of the 1600s, French traders began to build fur trading forts and posts along the banks of the St. Lawrence River. They also started **colonies** in the area. Samuel de Champlain, a French explorer, established a fur trading post at Quebec to control the fur trade along the St. Lawrence.

Other Europeans realized the fur trade could bring them riches as well. In 1670, the British jumped into the contest to build the largest fur trade company in North America. That year, King Charles II of Great Britain gave a group of **investors** control over all of the trade within the territory of the Hudson Bay **drainage basin**. This area, which included James Bay to the south of Hudson Bay, was called **Rupert's Land**. The investors called their company the Hudson's Bay Company in honour of the British explorer Henry Hudson, who discovered Hudson Bay.

Soon, trading posts operated by the British appeared along the shore of Hudson Bay. The first trading post was established at Moose Factory in 1673. Albany Fort, Severn House, and other trading posts were soon constructed. York Factory, which was to become one of the Hudson's Bay Company's main supply centres in the north, was established in 1684.

ABITATION.DE QVEBECQ

The trading post Champlain founded in 1608 is now Quebec City.

? **Ask Yourself**

How did the fur trade help to build what is now Canada?

Inside the Trading Post

Trading posts did not come in standard shapes and sizes. Sometimes a post was composed of only a small collection of wooden shacks on the banks of a river. These shacks housed several men who traded with the Aboriginal Peoples. The men also recorded how many beaver pelts were received and the items the Aboriginal Peoples traded for the pelts.

Other trading posts were much larger, housing as many as 500 people. In the centre of these posts, there was often a large building constructed in the shape of the letter "H." Smaller buildings surrounded the central building and were laid out in narrow rows that resembled streets. Wooden **palisades** that rose as high as five metres surrounded the entire area, which looked and functioned like a small town. Sometimes there were cannons mounted on the palisades.

Aboriginal traders set up teepees near trading posts.

At York Factory, the main depot, the guest house, and a summer **mess house** formed the centre bar of the H. The legs of the H held four fur stores, while the arms of the H contained the trading shop, **provisions** store, the clerks' quarters, and the house of the officer in charge. More than 50 buildings surrounded the central depot building. These included a hospital, a doctor's office, a schoolhouse, and a library. There were also workshops for carpenters, blacksmiths, and tinsmiths.

FIRST-HAND ACCOUNT

York Factory Houses

"It looks beautiful. The houses are painted pale yellow. The windows and some particular parts are white. Some have green gauze mosquito curtains outside and the effect is very good."

Letitia Hargrave, wife of James Hargrave, chief trader for the Hudson's Bay Company

Techniques of the Trade

Early trading posts were hastily erected. They were built of squared timber walls. Mud filled in the narrow spaces between the timbers to keep out the cold. The outside walls were whitewashed with white mud. Often, the bark from coniferous trees was used to make a roof. The windows were covered with animal skins, although this did not keep out the many insects that tormented the early traders at the posts in the northern regions.

A blacksmith's workshop had a forge to heat metal, a chimney to draw the smoke out of the room, and an anvil for the blacksmith to hammer and shape the metal.

MORE ON THE WEB

www.pc.gc.ca/lhn-hs/ab/rockymountain/natcul/natcul03_E.asp

Fort Vancouver was the headquarters of the Hudson's Bay Company's British Columbia department. The fort helped support nearby settlers throughout the winter months.

Life at the Trading Post

At the Hudson's Bay Company trading posts, a chief factor, or manager, and several other officers ran the post according to rules and regulations. These rules were made by the company's board of directors thousands of kilometres away across the ocean in Great Britain.

The posts were run with military precision. Employees who were not officers were called servants. A bell rang throughout the post at regular intervals to tell everyone what to do. The bell signalled what time to work and when to eat. At the end of the day, the ringing bell signalled that the night watchman must tend to his duties. All of the post's employees, from the highest ranked officer to the most inexperienced clerk, were expected to follow the rules.

Everyone had to work hard. Many of the clerks woke to the bell at five in the morning and worked until 10 o'clock at night. On Sunday, all the people in the post were expected to go to church.

Throughout the year, supply ships came from Great Britain to Hudson Bay with food for the traders. Salted meats, chocolate, flour, and oatmeal were sent by canoe or **york boat** to the trading posts in the interior of Canada. The men also hunted and fished to add more variety to their diet. Even small trading posts grew as many vegetables as possible during the short summer growing season.

Life at the forts was not all work. Each post had a Bachelor's Hall where the men could go to play cards and dice games or dance to the tunes of a fiddler.

FIRST-HAND ACCOUNT

Life at York Factory

"There are always between thirty and forty men resident at the post, summer and winter; generally four or five clerks, a post-master, and a skipper for the small schooners. The whole is under the direction and superintendence of a chief factor, or chief trader."

White bread and cheese were rare, luxury foods during the fur trade.

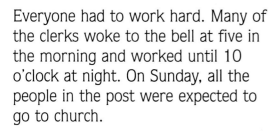

The Hudson's Bay Company established fur trading posts across Canada, from the Atlantic to the Pacific Ocean.

Defending the Posts

From the beginning of the fur trade, the British and French tried to gain a trade advantage over the other by building competing posts near bodies of water. While the Hudson's Bay Company quickly built posts around Hudson Bay, the French travelled farther inland and blocked the routes used by the Aboriginal traders to reach the Hudson's Bay Company posts.

This caused the flow of beaver pelts into the Hudson's Bay Company trading posts to dry up. The British realized they could no longer sit in their posts and wait for the Aboriginal Peoples to come to them. The Hudson's Bay Company was forced to venture farther inland, too.

Back in Europe, the British and French were fighting the Seven Years' War. The war extended to the colonies as well, including those in what is now Canada. Skirmishes broke out as the British and French fought for control of North America. The winning nation would also control the fur trade.

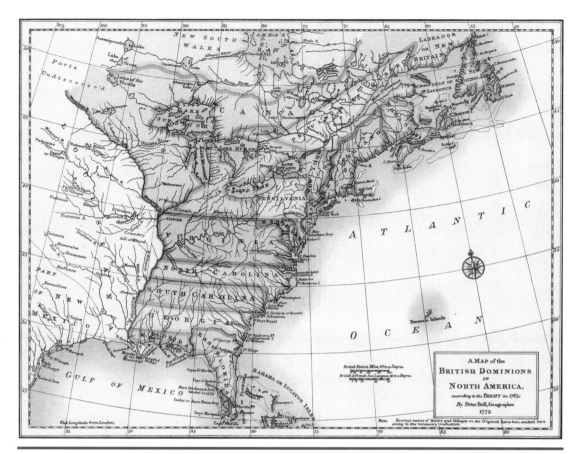

At the end of the Seven Years' War, Great Britain controlled parts of North America, as well as the fur trade.

To protect their traders, the British turned their posts into forts. Ownership of some forts changed back and forth between the rival countries. York Factory, the main depot for sending furs back to England, was burned to the ground by the French. York Factory was regained and rebuilt by the British, then attacked again several times.

The Seven Years' War

The Seven Years' War took place from 1756 to 1763 and involved several European countries. Great Britain sided with Prussia, a German kingdom, to fight against the countries of Austria, Russia, and France. In battling France, the British hoped to eliminate their trade rival by destroying the French navy and merchant fleet and taking control of the French colonies in North America. The British and French at the North American trading posts battled until 1763. That year, the French and British signed the Treaty of Paris. This treaty ended the Seven Years' War. Under the terms of the treaty, France gave Great Britain control of most of its land claims in what is now Canada. This allowed Great Britain's Hudson's Bay Company to expand its influence westward across the country.

The North West Company

From the outset of building trading posts on the shores of Hudson and James Bays, the Hudson's Bay Company faced competition from other traders. Its main rival was the North West Company. Founded in 1783, the North West Company was headquartered in Montreal. Its main post was at Fort William on Lake Superior. North West Company traders, or "Nor'Westers," as they were known, traded west of the Rocky Mountains and as far north as the Arctic.

Often, the founding of North West Company trading posts was followed by the construction of Hudson's Bay Company posts nearby. The competing posts were located within a "**musket**'s shot" of one another. For example, in 1795, the North West Company opened Fort Augustus on the Saskatchewan River. Several months later, the Hudson's Bay Company established Fort Edmonton in the same area. Locating competing posts close together was not good for either company. By bargaining between the posts,

The North West Company's motto was "Perseverance," which was written across the top of the company crest.

Aboriginal Peoples were able to push the price of furs up. As well, so many beaver were being hunted in the shared area that their numbers dwindled.

Neither company could prosper under these conditions. So, in 1821, they decided to join together under the name Hudson's Bay Company. From this time forward, the Hudson's Bay Company dominated the fur trade in North America. Its network of trading posts crossed present-day Canada from the Atlantic to the Pacific and up to the Arctic Ocean.

The Hudson's Bay Company is the oldest commercial corporation in North America.

FIRST-HAND ACCOUNT

Two Companies Merge

"The two sections of the guests, at summons of the bell, entered the great hall in silence, and kept wholly apart until the new governor moving in the throng with bows, smiles and introduction, brought about some conversation or hand-shaking between individuals, and ended by pointing at, politely, where he invited the guests to sit."

John Tod, Hudson's Bay Company employee

At one time, the icy shores of the Hudson Bay were home to many forts and trading posts.

Important Forts

York Factory

Located on the shores of Hudson Bay, York Factory was originally called York Fort. It was named for the Duke of York, a governor of the Hudson's Bay Company. Later he became King James II of Great Britain. The post was later called a "Factory" because the chief factor, the company's top employee in the region, lived at the post. Established in 1684, York Factory was the main depot for bringing manufactured goods into North America and shipping furs back to Great Britain. York Factory operated until 1957. At that time, the Hudson's Bay Company gave the post to the Canadian government. Today, York Factory is a national historic site.

Fort Edmonton

Built in 1795, Fort Edmonton was named for an estate in Great Britain owned by an investor in the Hudson's Bay Company. The fort was one of the Hudson's Bay Company's most successful fur trading posts. The success of the post was due to its location on the North Saskatchewan River near territories of the Blackfoot, Cree, Chipewyan, and Assiniboin people. After the merger of the North West Company and the Hudson's Bay Company, Fort Edmonton became the district headquarters for the North Saskatchewan region and served as a key supply depot. In 1915, after falling into decay, Fort Edmonton was demolished.

Lower Fort Garry

Located on the Red River in what is now Manitoba, Lower Fort Garry not only served as a trading post, but was also the administrative centre of the Hudson's Bay Company in the 1800s. Due to its location at the fork of the Red and Assiniboine Rivers, the fort also became the community hub of the Red River Settlement, a colony made up mainly of British settlers. By the 1860s, Lower Fort Garry developed into an industrial centre with flour mills, sawmills, and blacksmith shops. In the mid-1900s, Lower Fort Garry was designated a national historic site, and it attracts many visitors each year.

Fort William

In 1803, the North West Company built Fort William at the mouth of the Kaministiquia River near what is now Thunder Bay, Ontario. The fort served as the company's headquarters and was the site of its annual summer **rendezvous** for the company's traders and trappers. The fort ceased operating after the North West Company's merger with the Hudson's Bay Company and was later demolished. In 1971, the Ontario government reconstructed the fort. Fort William is now a popular tourist destination in Thunder Bay.

Furs were delivered to Lower Fort Garry until the early twentieth century.

Aboriginal Peoples and the Trading Posts

Every summer, the trading posts were a beehive of activity as Aboriginal Peoples came to trade beaver pelts and other furs in exchange for European manufactured goods. Before the actual trading commenced, there were often elaborate ceremonies to honour the ongoing trade relationship.

Gifts of tobacco and other items were often exchanged between trading partners.

Aboriginal trade parties dressed in their best attire approached the fort in canoes. The canoe that held the trade captain flew a flag to indicate his status. As the canoes came in sight of the trading posts, the traders fired rifles in the air. A welcome boom from the post's guns answered, echoing through the air. Onshore, Aboriginal men and women unloaded their furs, while their captains met with the highest officials at the post.

Over the next several days, peace pipes were smoked, stories told, and feasts held. Then, on behalf of their people, the captains traded their pelts for the European goods. At leave taking, gifts were exchanged along with promises to meet again the next year at the post.

In the early days of the fur trade, each trading post set its own rate of exchange for trading. Aboriginal traders naturally wanted the highest price for their furs. They often went to more than one trading post to see what the traders there would pay. This meant that some posts did more business than others. In time, the Hudson's Bay Company decided to standardize the exchange rate. This helped stabilize trade between posts.

FIRST-HAND ACCOUNT

Trading Room at York Factory

"The trading-room…contained every imaginable commodity likely to be needed…On various shelves were piled bales of cloth of all colours, capotes, blankets, caps, etc.; and in smaller divisions were placed files, scalping-knives, gun-screws, flints, balls of twine, fire-steels, canoe-awls, and glass beads of all colours, sizes, and descriptions."

"Drawers in the counter contained needles, pins, scissors, thimbles, fish-hooks, and vermilion for painting canoes and faces. The floor was strewn with a variety of copper and tin kettles, from half-a-pint to a gallon; and on a stand in the furthest corner of the room stood about a dozen trading guns, and beside them a keg of powder and a box of shot."

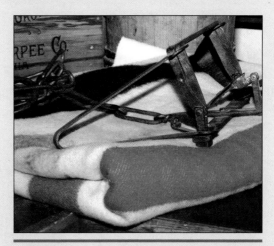

Blankets were a popular Hudson's Bay Company trading item.

 Ask Yourself

How did standardizing the exchange rate help stabilize trade?

How Women Contributed

Aboriginal women worked as unofficial employees of fur trade companies. They served as guides, interpreters, and as part of the work crew on trade expeditions. The work women performed at remote posts, including hunting for small game and collecting vegetation, ensured the survival of company employees.

In the early days of the fur trade, there were very few non-Aboriginal women at the trading posts. Most of the fur traders and other employees of the Hudson's Bay Company or North West Company were young men who were not married.

Often, fur traders married Aboriginal Peoples, and later, **Métis** women. The marriages often strengthened the ties between the fur traders and the Aboriginal Peoples by fostering good trade relations between the women's families and their husbands. The women also helped in more direct ways by teaching employees at the post many skills needed to survive in the wilderness. In turn, the Aboriginal

Aboriginal women who married European fur traders were called "country wives."

Peoples had a source of information about life at the posts and trading.

Unfortunately, the officials in Great Britain did not always recognize the contributions of Aboriginal women. In 1802, Hudson's Bay Company officials in Great Britain decided not to pay for clothing for the employees' Aboriginal wives. This decision angered the fur traders and clerks, who told the officials about their wives' important contributions to the daily activities of the trading posts.

FIRST-HAND ACCOUNT

Description of a Country Wife's Work

"The women are deserving of some encouragement and indulgence from your Honors, they clean and put into a state of preservation all Beavr. and Otter skins ... They prepare Line for Snow shoes and knit them also without which your Honors servants could not give efficient opposition to the Canadian traders they make Leather shoes for the men who are obliged to travel ... and are useful in a variety of other instances, in short they are Virtually your Honors Servants."

Thanadelthur

Thanadelthur was a Chipewyan woman whose courage and resourcefulness helped the Hudson's Bay Company expand the fur trade into the area north of York Factory.

In 1713, as a teenager, Thanadelthur was captured by a rival Cree group. With the help of some fur traders, she escaped the next year during a very harsh winter. She made her way to the York Factory trading post to rest until spring. There, Thanadelthur told Chief Factor James Knight that her people wanted to trade furs with them. The problem was that the Cree had guns and were waging war on the Chipewyan. She also told Knight about the abundance of furs and a copper mine in the northwest, beyond the Churchill River.

Excited by her tales, Knight organized an expedition of traders and Chipewyan to map and explore the Churchill River area. He asked Thanadelthur, who spoke both Chipewyan and Cree, to act as the guide and interpreter. They embarked on the dangerous journey that took more than a year. Many times the group ran out of food and had to eat snow to survive. They were also attacked by the Cree. Thanadelthur did not give up. She convinced the Cree and Chipewyan to make peace.

On her return to York Factory, Thanadelthur taught her people which furs the British most valued. She showed them how to prepare the furs to fetch the highest price. Although she died of a fever the next winter, Thanadelthur's role in the peace mission earned her respect from both Aboriginal Peoples and British fur traders.

Fur Trade Personalities

George Simpson

George Simpson was governor of the Hudson's Bay Company in Rupert's Land from 1826 to 1860. During this period, the North West Company merged with the Hudson's Bay Company to form one huge fur trading enterprise. Simpson's job was to make the new company **profitable**.

Simpson was a smart, efficient businessman. Some people called him strict, but they all agreed he was fair. He closed posts in areas where there were too many. He told the chief factors to keep detailed records of each trade in an account book. Simpson made surprise visits to the trading posts to check on the employees. He travelled by canoe with an escort of Aboriginal guides. He was a colourful personality who wore a top hat in the wilderness. He used to come ashore at the posts accompanied by his own personal bagpiper.

George Simpson had fur traders travel by york boat rather than canoe because canoes could carry more supplies.

In 1841, Simpson was knighted by Queen Victoria of Great Britain for his accomplishments. He worked for the Hudson's Bay Company until his death in 1860. He is buried in Montreal.

James Douglas

James Douglas is known as the Father of British Columbia. He came to Canada as an apprentice clerk with the North West Company when he was only 16 years old. Douglas travelled in a canoe to Fort William with a company of **voyageurs**. Fort William was the main supply depot for the company's fur trading posts in the west. After the North West Company was absorbed by the Hudson's Bay Company, Douglas was sent farther west to Fort St. James. Later, he was promoted to the position of chief factor of Fort Vancouver on the Columbia River.

In 1846, Great Britain and the United States agreed upon a boundary at the 49th parallel. This arrangement placed Fort Vancouver in Oregon on the United States side of the border. Douglas was told to find a new headquarters for the Hudson's Bay Company's Pacific fur trade. In 1849, he established Fort Victoria on Vancouver Island.

Douglas later resigned from the Hudson's Bay Company to devote his energies full time to politics. When mainland British Columbia became an official colony in 1858, he was appointed its governor. In 1864, Douglas retired as governor. Queen Victoria knighted him for his services to British Columbia. He lived the rest of his life in Victoria.

Queen Victoria was the longest reigning monarch in Great Britain's history.

The Rise and Fall of the Beaver

The fate and fortune of the trading posts depended on the fur trade, especially on the availability and quality of beaver pelts. Not all of the trading posts operated year-round. In some areas, posts were closed in the summer when only inferior summer pelts were available.

Before the fur trade, there were more than six million beaver in Canada.

Hat-makers preferred beaver skins that had been worn for a year or more because they produced better felt.

Before the merger of the North West Company and the Hudson's Bay Company, competition for beaver pelts sometimes caused over-trapping. The beaver population began to decline. The number of Aboriginal traders bringing pelts to the posts declined also, as the trappers moved on to other areas where beaver was more plentiful. During these periods, unprofitable posts were closed, some temporarily and some permanently.

By the 1840s, the Hudson's Bay Company decided on a program of **conservation**. It voluntarily closed some of its posts in specific areas to allow the beaver population to rebuild.

In time, the beaver hat began to lose its appeal in Europe as silk hats became the sought-after item for fashionable gentlemen.

The Hudson's Bay Company began building department stores across Canada in the late 1800s.

The Fur Trade Today

By the 1870s, changing tastes in European fashion resulted in less demand for beaver pelts and other furs. At the same time, Canada's population was growing. Towns and cities were springing up near trading posts. This presented a new opportunity for the Hudson's Bay Company. Slowly, the company converted its trading posts into retail stores that sold a wide variety of goods. In 1881, the company opened its first modern department store in Winnipeg, Manitoba.

The Hudson's Bay Company shifted its focus to furs other than beaver. It set up new trading posts in the western Arctic, where it traded with the Aboriginal Peoples for muskrat and fox furs. As late as the 1950s, the company still advertised

for fur traders to work at its posts in the Arctic.

By 1987, most of the original trading posts had become retail stores. The Hudson's Bay Company decided to focus on developing its business in southern Canada. It sold its stores in northern Canada to a group of investors, many of whom were Hudson's Bay Company employees. Remembering the courage and adventure of the early fur traders, they named their new company the North West Company. Today, some of the new company's stores continue the legacy of the trade relationship between Aboriginal Peoples and fur traders by selling Aboriginal handicrafts and furs.

In the 1940s, fur coats sold at Hudson's Bay Company stores were considered quite fashionable.

Timeline

1666 Radisson and Des Groseilliers travel to London, where Prince Rupert sponsors them to begin fur explorations around Hudson Bay.

1668 On a fur-finding mission, two ships leave from London. The *Eaglet* is forced to turn back, but the *Nonsuch* reaches Hudson Bay.

1669 The *Nonsuch* returns to England with a cargo of furs.

1670 King Charles II grants a group of investors a Royal Charter, called the "Governor and Company of Adventurers of England Trading into Hudson Bay," or the Hudson's Bay Company.

1673 Moose Factory is established in present-day Ontario.

1679 Albany Fort is founded in present-day Ontario.

1680 Severn House is established in present-day Ontario.

1684 York Factory is built in present-day Manitoba.

1690 Henry Kelsey begins a two-year journey to explore the Prairies.

1713 As part of the Treaty of Utrecht, France gives up all claims to Hudson Bay.

1754 Anthony Henday travels inland from York Factory to trade with Aboriginal Peoples. He goes as far as the Prairies and meets the Blackfoot.

1774 Samuel Hearne builds the first inland post near Pine Island Lake, called Cumberland House, in present-day Saskatchewan.

1783 The North West Company, founded in Montreal, becomes a rival to the Hudson's Bay Company.

1795 Fort Edmonton is established.

1803 The North West Company opens a fur exchange at Lachine, near Montreal.

1821 The Hudson's Bay Company and the North West Company merge. By this time, the Hudson's Bay Company operates 173 posts and controls 7.7 million square kilometres of land.

1825 Fort Vancouver is founded along the Columbia River in today's province of British Columbia.

1827 Fort Langley is established in present-day British Columbia.

1831 Lower Fort Garry is founded in present-day Manitoba.

1843 Fort Victoria is built in present-day British Columbia.

1869 In the Deed of Surrender, the Hudson's Bay Company returns ownership of Rupert's Land to Great Britain, which then grants it to the new country of Canada.

1881 The Hudson's Bay Company opens its first department store in Winnipeg.

1915–19 To help during World War I, the Hudson's Bay Company charters 300 ocean vessels to carry food, fuel, lumber, and munitions.

1930 Beaver populations decline in northern Quebec. More than 18,000 square kilometres of land are leased for their protection.

2006 The Hudson's Bay Company is sold to U.S. businessman Jerry Zucker.

Test Your Knowledge

As explorers mapped out Canada, trading posts were established to take advantage of the growing fur trade. The posts were located from the shores of the St. Lawrence River overland to the area west of the Rocky Mountains. Settlers lived near many of the trading posts. In time, these communities became growing towns and cities. For more than 300 years, much of Canada's economic activity revolved around the fur trade.

QUESTIONS

1. Create a diagram of an "H-shaped" trading post. Include a plan of the rooms people used for their daily living. Add in areas for rooms used for trading and other business activities. Draw and label where community buildings might be located. Where might a garden be placed?

2. Why was beaver fur so popular in Europe? What caused the popularity of beaver pelts to decline? What impact did this have on the fur trade in Canada?

3. The fur trading companies established a network of trading posts throughout Canada's North and interior. Furs were sent from small posts to larger ones, where the furs were sorted and shipped to Great Britain. Draw an idea web that connects the elements required to successfully send furs from remote inland posts to York Factory on Hudson Bay. What kind of transportation would be required on the water? How would the furs be transported overland?

More Information

How can I find more information about the fur trade?

Libraries have many interesting books about forts and trading posts.

Museums are great places to learn about the fur trade. The Internet offers some great websites dedicated to the fur trade.

Where can I find a good reference website to learn more about forts and trading posts?

Hudson's Bay Company
www.hbc.com/hbcheritage/history

The North West Company
www.northwest.ca

Fur Trade Stories
www.furtradestories.ca

Words to Know

colonies: places where people come to settle

conservation: protecting from harm or loss

drainage basin: the area of land rivers flow toward, or empty into

investors: people who spend money on something expecting it to make a profit later

mess house: a building where people eat meals

Métis: a person of mixed Aboriginal and European descent

musket: a muzzle-loading shoulder gun with a long barrel

palisades: towers built along a fort wall that allow for clear views of surrounding area or places to mount weapons for defence

portaged: carried a canoe overland until the next river or stream

profitable: successful at making money

provisions: supplies

rendezvous: an annual meeting of fur traders

Rupert's Land: the area that drained into Hudson Bay; nearly 4 million square kilometres of land between Labrador and the Rocky Mountains

voyageurs: boatmen or guides employed by a fur trade company to transport goods and supplies between trading posts

york boat: a flat-bottomed boat with a pointed bow that could carry three times as much cargo as the largest birchbark canoe

Index

Aboriginal Peoples 5, 8, 12, 15, 18, 19, 20, 21, 22, 25, 27, 28

beaver 5, 8, 12, 15, 18, 24, 25, 26, 27, 29, 30

country wives 20, 21

Douglas, James 23

Fort Edmonton 5, 15, 16, 28

Fort William 4, 17, 23

Hudson's Bay Company 5, 7, 9, 10, 12, 13, 14, 15, 16, 17, 19, 20, 21, 22, 23, 25, 26, 27, 28, 29

Lower Fort Garry 17, 29

North West Company 14, 15, 16, 17, 20, 22, 23, 25, 27, 28, 29, 34

Rupert's Land 7, 22, 29

Simpson, George 22

York Factory 9, 11, 13, 16, 19, 21, 28, 30